A 31-DAY PRAYER DEVOTIONAL FOR THE MEN IN YOUR LIFE

TRACY SPENCER

Copyright © 2020
ISBN 978-0-9966804-3-1
Cover Design by Tracy Spencer

All rights reserved. No part of this publication may be reproduced, stored, or transmitted in any form or by any means, electronic, mechanical, photocopying, recording, scanning, or otherwise, except as permitted under Section 107 or 108 of the 1976 United States Copyright Act, without the prior written permission of the author. Requests to the author and publisher for permission should be addressed to the following email: TracyGSpencer@gmail.com

Limitation of liability/disclaimer of warranty: While the publisher and author have used their best efforts in providing helpful and useful content in this book, they make no representations or warranties with respect to the accuracy or completeness of the contents of this document and specifically disclaim any implied warranties of merchantability or fitness for particular purpose.

The advice and strategies contained therein may not be suitable for your situation. You should consult with a professional where appropriate. Neither the publisher nor author shall be liable for any loss of health, profit or any other commercial damages, including but not limited to special, incidental, consequential, or other damages.

DEDICATION

This book is dedicated to my best friend, confidante, love, and husband, Duane. In a season of my own personal struggles and grief, God directed my attention to you, and guided me to intercede for you. They say that prayer changes things, but prayer changed ME!! My life has been forever changed. I love you with an everlasting love. I would also like to dedicate this book to our children—DJ, Eric, Ryan Elise, and Kailey. I love you, cherish you, and I will never stop praying for you. And lastly, this book is dedicated to my mother, Alfria, and to the unforgettable memory of my father, Curtis Grady. I dedicate this to your legacy and all who are connected. Thank you both for teaching me the importance of prayer.

Dedication

ACKNOWLEDGEMENTS

First things first—this book would not be a thought without the leading of the Holy Spirit. I thank God for placing this project in my heart.

For the development and production of this book, I would like to extend my sincere gratitude to:

My husband and forever love, Duane, and my children. It is my honor to do life with you. Thank you for not allowing me to give up.

Dr. Beverly Crockett and Julie Boney. I can't thank you enough for your help in making this project come to pass.

My dear mother, Alfria and my sisters, Betty, Bernice, Brenda (my prayer partner), and LaTussia. I love you all!

There are many people to whom I owe a tremendous level of gratitude (and I know that I will miss someone)— Olive Spencer (Nana), Duana Spencer, Kendra Burton-Tennyson, Kiyanah Miles (finding your old email was golden), Stephanie Johnson-Creswell, Sheryl Adams, Cynthia Norwood, Wanda Thompson, Regina Morris, Sabrina Clayvon, Chrystalyn Hawthorne, Barbara Stroud, Lakeisha Spencer, Kismet Evans, Grace Myers, Syrenthia Haley, Mimi Hawkins. Your love, loyalty, and support for my family and for who I am in God gives me strength.

Acknowledgements

My circle of support, my Grady family, my End Time Ministries family, my #Prayer21 family, my Mississippi family, my Florida family, my California family, and all who have kindly supported me and my family in ministry and who have joined with me in intercession over the years. God bless and keep you all. Much love.

cov·er
/ˈkəvər/
verb
1. put something such as a cloth or lid on top of or in front of (something) in order to protect or conceal it.
"her husband had been covered with prayer"
2. extend over (an area).
"his prayer covered the entire football team"

noun
1. a thing which lies on, over, or around something, especially in order to protect or conceal it.
"a prayer cover"
2. physical shelter or protection sought by people in danger.
"the sirens wailed and the people sought the LORD for cover"

Cover Him

INTRODUCTION

Why should we cover him?

There has been a rift in our society regarding the value of men. Whether by way of a lack of self-worth or a depreciation of value amongst people in general, the perpetrated rift is not limited to relationship status, age, class, race, religion nor affiliation. On top of that, statistics show that a growing number of adolescent boys are experiencing depression with at least two major episodes (visible breakdowns) with no treatment or helpful intervention. There are strategic tactics and plots which seek to kill, steal, and destroy. One such tactic is when someone is made to feel that they have to manage life under their own strength. We tend to hold men at a standard where self-strength is the only option, with no room to express moments of weakness. One of the most flawed misconceptions concerning prayer is that people who appear to be resilient are not in need of prayer as much as others. We all need prayer.

Intercession is without doubt a powerful benefit to believers everywhere, but it requires an investment of time, sacrifice, and commitment. We all recognize that time is indeed a precious commodity often wasted. In the case of intercession, time is a multi-yielding act of goodness that is

Introduction

never wasted. When we pray for the needs of others, the Holy Spirit will strengthen us in the process. Intercession is a posture of humility where we go to God in relentless pursuit of breakthrough for others. Intercession is a position of focus, as we choose to see what God says over what we see. Intercession is a place where we find God opening doors for us at moments where we least expected because we choose to place others before Him in prayer just as if their needs were our own.

In 2 Corinthians we are urged not to wage war from a carnal perspective, but to wage war in the spirit as the bible says the weapons of our warfare are not of flesh, but they are divinely empowered by God to destroy strongholds. But there is a qualifier attached to this. In order that we might access these divinely empowered arsenals, we must commit our lives to be obedient to God and His Word. So, if we have not fulfilled our obedience to God, we should not expect to hand Him a list of "honey-do's" and expect Him to "get 'er done." And I will be the first to say that God has come through for me even in my disobedience because He is Sovereign, but if we intend to stand according to all He has ordained for us then we must take up our own cross and follow His precepts as disciples and not be content with a daily walk of flesh as our flesh must be crucified daily. It is our purpose to stand in the power of God as we behold the breaking of chains.

In this devotional, our focus is on prayer and action. Each day will feature an area focus of prayer, along with a bible-based prayer and an action plan. The application of the action plan is at your discretion, so do what you feel led to do. Prayerfully consider choosing a time of day where you can pray and listen. Not only will we intercede for the men in our lives, we will take action as we are led by the Holy Spirit, and we will expect God to do great things. Remember, nothing is too difficult for God.

Again, why should we cover him?? The answer is simple. We should cover him because God said we should cover each other in prayer and because he needs to be covered. We have already experienced enough negativity, ridicule, and judgment towards men in general. Many of us know what it feels like to be kicked while we're down. In moments of vulnerability, we need a safe place of covering to be healed and delivered. The only true covering that can protect him, shield him, conceal him, and shelter him is found in God alone. Prayer is our access to God, and we utilize His Word as our foundation for our prayers. Praying God's Word allows us to agree with what He has already established. When we pray God's Word over *him,* we can trust that our Sovereign God will cover him completely.

God allowed me to see the importance of intercession while I was experiencing undue stress on the job, mental

Introduction

anguish from a toxic workplace, being bullied in the same toxic workplace, battling with depression and low self-esteem—all this, combined with debilitating health issues, anxiety, and the terminal illness and subsequent death of my father. My husband was interceding for me, working full time, doing full time ministry, and holding our family together through my struggles. I didn't have the strength to pray for myself, but God knew that I would give all that I had for someone I loved, so He led me to intercede for my husband whom I love with my whole heart. It was through intercession for him that God moved for me also. Not only did I intercede for my husband, I invited others on several occasions to intercede for their husbands, their sons, their fathers, their brothers, and by God's grace, there were thousands who stood together praying God's Word on social media.

If you have a husband or a son, an uncle or a nephew, a father or a cousin, a neighbor or a friend— whether that man is a newborn or seasoned in age, this devotional is meant for you. As you devote this time of prayer, I pray that God will bless you abundantly for your labor of love. Remember, there is nothing like a prayer and a plan!

Day 1
SALVATION

Our first day in prayer is our most important day. As we pray, we are keeping our eyes upon God's Word for guidance as the Holy Spirit leads. We are starting our prayer journey with salvation for a few reasons. Firstly, salvation is freedom from the bondages of sin, and we want that freedom for each person we cover in prayer. The bible says in Mark 8:36, "For what shall it profit a man, if he shall gain the whole world, and lose his own soul?" We need a soul check on behalf of those that we love and care about.

We can own the finest homes in the world and have money to burn, but if we have not accepted the redemptive gift of salvation through Christ Jesus, we have nothing. There is no lasting latitude in how much you own or how famous you become. The only lasting wealth is found by having

Day 1

relationship with God by way of salvation through Christ Jesus.

All the tangible things we consider to be of value require some form of work to obtain. On the other hand, salvation cannot be bought or sold. It is a gift from God Himself. Before we ask God for anything measurable, let us ask God for the ultimate and immeasurable gift of salvation for our husbands, fathers, fiancés, sons, brothers, and for all the men in our lives.

This poor man cried, and the LORD heard him, and saved him out of all his troubles. Psalm 34:6

PRAYER

Dear Jesus, I ask You for Your love and kindness to manifest in the heart of _____ for the saving of his soul. LORD, save _____, cleanse him from all unrighteousness, and give him faith to believe and receive all that You have provided for him. Let the message of the Gospel of Jesus Christ penetrate his heart and cause his faith to respond to Your love. Lead _____ to confess with his mouth and believe in his heart that You died and rose from the grave to save him. LORD, help _____ to understand that Your salvation brings true deliverance, wholeness, and preservation in every area of his life. Holy Spirit, do a mighty work within the life of _____. LORD, You said in Your Word that whoever calls upon Your name will be saved. Save _____ and release him from the bondages of sin. Be the Lord of his life in Jesus' name. Amen.

PRAYER REQUESTS/PRAISE REPORTS

_____

_____

_____

_____

_____

Day 1

ACTION PLAN

PRAISE — Praise God for salvation for the one (s) you have prayed for.

REFLECT — Reflect upon the moment you received Christ.

ACT — Share the hope of salvation with someone.

YIELD — Meditate on the scriptures below.

SUPPORTING SCRIPTURES

John 3:16 – For God so loved the world, that he gave his only begotten Son, that whosoever believeth in him should not perish, but have everlasting life.

Romans 10:9 –That if thou shalt confess with thy mouth the Lord Jesus, and shalt believe in thine heart that God hath raised him from the dead, thou shalt be saved.

Romans 10:13 – For whosoever shall call upon the name of the Lord shall be saved.

Day 2
WISDOM

The power of knowledge can be futile if wisdom is not applied. How many times have you openly shared what you knew, but the timing was terrible? Or how many times have you witnessed someone who had all the answers to a problem, yet they did not know how to apply those answers for results. The stereotypical picture of men is that they have knowledge and information, but they are unwilling to seek guidance. Sort of how we see the all too familiar TV scene of the man trying to assemble the bicycle while refusing to read the "how-to" manual. If we are honest with ourselves, we would admit that this is not a singled-out issue reserved for men only. We have all been there at some point, and after a

Day 2

few stumbles of trying to do things on our own, we realize that we need God's wisdom.

As you pray for the men in your life, let your faith connect to one of God's most pivotal precepts. The Word of God tells us in Proverbs 4:7 that "wisdom is the principal thing." Without Godly wisdom and understanding, all our efforts are beating against the wind. We may not have all the knowledge we desire, but we can rely upon God's wisdom to guide us even when we do not know the "what" or the "how."

Continue in prayer, and watch in the same with thanksgiving.
Colossians 4:2

PRAYER

Abba, Your Word says that if I ask You for anything according to Your Word, You hear me. I ask You to draw _____ to You through Your love and kindness. LORD, give _____ the understanding to realize that wisdom from You is the principle virtue for life's journey. Give _____ the boldness to ask You for a liberal supply of wisdom. LORD, give him understanding in all matters that pertain to life and godliness. Help _____ make sound decisions based upon Your counsel and not his own understanding. Surround him with other men who love You and cling to Your wisdom. Release the true riches of Your wisdom to him and let him find joy unspeakable in the wisdom that comes from You alone. In Jesus' name. Amen.

PRAYER REQUESTS/PRAISE REPORTS

_____
_____
_____
_____
_____
_____

Day 2

ACTION PLAN

PRAISE
Praise God for a liberal supply of wisdom each day.

REFLECT
Reflect upon a time when God's wisdom helped you.

ACT
Share a word of Godly wisdom with someone.

YIELD
Meditate on the scriptures below.

SUPPORTING SCRIPTURES

James 1:5 – If any of you lacks wisdom, he should ask God, who gives generously to all without finding fault, and it will be given to him.

Proverbs 4:7 – Wisdom is the principal thing; therefore get wisdom: and with all thy getting get understanding.

Proverbs 3:13 – Blessed is the one who finds wisdom, and the one who gets understanding,

Day 3
PURE HEART

Our society at-large has not been a favorable contributor to purity. The enemy has spearheaded an agenda which seeks to desensitize the hearts and minds of men as early in life as possible. In fact, David reminds us in Psalm 51:5 that even he was 'shaped in iniquity, and in sin, his mother conceived him.' Even if one lived under a rock, in a cave in uncharted territory, there are external elements coupled with spiritual wickedness in high places which seek to taint the hearts of men.

The enemy will use whatever is available to him, in order to corrupt the heart; books, substances, TV, movies, music, social media, friends, and yes, even family. The adage says, "garbage in—garbage out," but it is our prayer that God will purify the hearts of our brothers, sons, husbands, fathers, and all the men in our lives.

Day 3

PRAYER

Father God, I thank You for _____. I ask You to purify his heart and sanctify him. LORD, You said in Your Word that those who place their hope in You will be purified. LORD, set _____ free from the stain of iniquity, and give him a clean heart which seeks after You. I pray that his intentions will be filled with love, goodness, compassion, mercy, and grace. Father God teach _____ how to turn away from deceitful deeds, and make him a vessel of honor, fit and pleasing to You. I plead the covenant blood of Jesus against all impure influences upon his life. Help _____ to see himself as You desire him to be; sanctified by the power of Your Spirit. In Jesus' name. Amen.

PRAYER REQUESTS/PRAISE REPORTS

_____
_____
_____
_____
_____
_____
_____

ACTION PLAN

PRAISE
Praise God for the cleansing blood of Christ Jesus.

REFLECT
Reflect on the delivering power of God's grace in your life.

ACT
Share a testimony of God's deliverance with someone.

YIELD
Meditate on the scriptures below.

SUPPORTING SCRIPTURES

Psalm 51:10 – Create in me a clean heart, O God, and renew a steadfast spirit within me.

2 Timothy 2:21 – Therefore, if anyone cleanses himself from what is dishonorable, he will be a vessel for honorable use, set apart as holy, useful to the master of the house, ready for every good work.

1 John 3:3 – And every man that hath this hope in him purifieth himself, even as he is pure.

Day 3

Day 4
FAITH

The men in your life are bound to have some measure of struggles in life, whether seen or unseen. There are also seen and unseen enemies at work, whose main goal is to redirect them from anything God has for them by way of distractions, deceptions, misguided actions, and loose priorities. Faith is the core of our belief in God, and all of those tactics are used both subtly and blatantly to undermine our faith.

Whenever a house is on fire, homeowners scramble to grab the items that they hold most precious and essential, with the hopes of saving as much as they can. Sometimes those same homeowners tend to forget one of the most precious items in the house is their own lives. Material things can be replaced, but life is an irreplaceable gift. We are going to treat

Day 4

faith in the same likeness, for faith is the catalyst which ignites a believer's hope – it is precious and essential!

Many of us are in a posture of prayer right now, due to the prayers of others on our behalf. That person who prayed for you realized that your life in Christ Jesus was meaningful, and they prayed for you when you could not pray for yourself. They saw the importance of faith in God and they cried out to God for you because of the importance of having faith in God. All of the promises of God are received by faith in who He is. Hebrews 11:6 says, "without faith it is impossible to please God, because anyone who comes to Him must believe that He exists and that He rewards those who earnestly seek Him."

Therefore, I say unto you, What things soever ye desire, when ye pray, believe that ye receive them, and ye shall have them. Mark 11:24

PRAYER

Father God, I pray for _____ to be a man of Godly faith. I ask You to strengthen _____ to trust You for guidance through the issues of life. LORD, provide every opportunity for _____ to confirm his freedom to walk in Your precepts and overcoming faith, through the fullness of salvation in Christ Jesus. LORD, help _____ to know that no substance, no counterfeit, no substitute, nor any ungodly thing can ever take the place of Your power at work in his life. Father, I ask that You fill him with the knowledge of Your will in all spiritual wisdom and understanding. Reveal Yourself to _____ as the true and living God who justifies by faith, and not works. Help _____ to walk in a way which pleases You. Let _____ bring glory to You as his life becomes fruitful in You. In Jesus' name I pray. Amen.

PRAYER REQUESTS/PRAISE REPORTS

_____

_____

_____

_____

_____

Day 4

ACTION PLAN

PRAISE — Praise God for providing faith to the one(s) you've prayed for.

REFLECT — Reflect on the power of faith at work in your life.

ACT — Listen to one of your favorites songs about faith.

YIELD — Meditate on the scriptures below.

SUPPORTING SCRIPTURES

Hebrews 11:1 – Now faith is being sure of what we hope for and certain of what we do not see.

Hebrews 11:6 – But without faith it is impossible to please him: for he that cometh to God must believe that he is, and that he is a rewarder of them that diligently seek him.

Ephesians 6:16 – Above all, taking the shield of faith, wherewith ye shall be able to quench all the fiery darts of the wicked

Day 5
INTEGRITY

Today we pray for integrity, for integrity is the litmus test to our motives and actions as well as the balancing scales to our character. It separates the holy from the hypocrite. Integrity gives one the ability to take the high road even when the low road is convenient and often profitable.

There was a young man who had finally found a job after being unemployed for months. He walked seven miles to work each day because he had no transportation. He would arrive early before the rest of the workers and he would stay after his shift was done so that he could walk home and avoid the mocking and sneers that were sure to come from his fellow employees. One day as he was leaving work for the weekend, he stumbled upon a brown envelope in the parking lot outside and when he looked inside, he saw several rolls of cash. With the door locked and everyone gone, he had no way of notifying anyone regarding what he had found; not to mention, his cellphone services were interrupted. The young man picked up the envelope and tucked it in his jacket and made the long trek home. He spent the entire weekend with the envelope without taking a dime of it, knowing that he could easily keep the money for himself, or buy a car— maybe even quit that job on Monday and find another. The young man returned to work on Monday and reported every penny of the money to his boss. The boss was relieved because the envelope had fallen from her secretary's belongings as she left work. It was fundraiser funds from the company's charity event. To show thanks for the young man's deeds, he was awarded $10,000 from the head of the company and his boss gifted him a new car.

Who are we when no one is watching? What are our actions when we are behind closed doors? Are we of the mindset that since we can't see anyone it means that we can't be seen? Do we preserve our ethical and moral standards in a consistent manner even when no one is watching? Yessss....a man of integrity.

PRAYER

Father God, Your Word says that those who walk in integrity will walk securely and I ask this for _____. I lift _____ before You and I ask that You lead and guide him to a place of Your truth. Let the benefits of a life of integrity speak to _____ and shape his Godly morals and character. Show _____ the way to righteousness by the leading of the Holy Spirit. Give _____ the courage to stand with integrity even when it is uncomfortable or unpopular. Thank You for hiding Your Word deep within _____ so that he will not sin against You. Father God, surround _____ with believers who walk in integrity as an example of how You preserve the upright. LORD, help _____ to think on things that are true, holy, just, loving, honorable and commendable. Be glorified in his life in Jesus' name. Amen.

PRAYER REQUESTS/PRAISE REPORTS

_____

_____

_____

_____

_____

Day 5

ACTION PLAN

PRAY

PRAISE – Praise God for showing you how to have integrity.

REFLECT – Reflect on a moment when your integrity made a difference.

ACT – Pray about any area in your life that compromises your integrity.

YIELD – Meditate on the scriptures below.

SUPPORTING SCRIPTURES

Proverbs 10:9 – Whoever walks in integrity walks securely, but he who makes his ways crooked will be found out.

Philippians 4:8 – Finally, brothers, whatever is true, whatever is honorable, whatever is just, whatever is pure, whatever is lovely, whatever is commendable, if there is any excellence, if there is anything worthy of praise, think about these things.

Psalm 25:21 – May integrity and uprightness preserve me, for I wait for you.

Day 6
COMMUNICATION

We all have challenges with communication to some degree - perhaps daily. Maybe we know what to say, but our delivery might be a bit sour. Sometimes we use toxic communication skills that we have learned from childhood, but we never realized the importance of fixing our broken communication skills. Communication is not only the means by which we exchange information, it is the way we maintain relationships. Communication includes, but is not limited to our words, facial expressions, dispositions, body language, actions, listening, or the lack of these elements altogether. The way we manage these skills can make or break a relationship.

One of the most powerful scriptures on communications is found in Ephesians 4:29 and it is clearly understood in the Amplified version: "Let no foul or polluting

Day 6

language, nor evil word nor unwholesome or worthless talk [ever] come out of your mouth, but only such [speech] as is good and beneficial to the spiritual progress of others, as is fitting to the need and the occasion, that it may be a blessing and give grace (God's favor) to those who hear it." So, when we pray today let us believe God for an abundant heart filled with grace.

Then shall ye call upon me, and ye shall go and pray unto me, and I will hearken unto you. Jeremiah 29:12

PRAYER

Father God, I thank You for creating _____ in Your likeness, with the capacity for clear thoughts and impactful communications which are acceptable in Your sight, oh LORD. I pray that _____ will be able to effectively communicate his thoughts, ideas, information, passions, emotions, and love. LORD, give _____ words of grace for all who hear him and cause his words to build up and not tear down. Let him be quick to listen, confident in speech, and considerate in response. Help _____ to refrain from speaking contrary to Your will. Father, Your Word declares that death and life are in the power of the tongue. Let _____ realize the power of his words and guide his mouth to speak blessing and not cursing. LORD, fill him with truth and grace and let him be blessed by the words he speaks. In Jesus' name I pray. Amen.

PRAYER REQUESTS/PRAISE REPORTS

_____

_____

_____

_____

_____

Day 6

ACTION PLAN

PRAISE
Praise God for an abundant heart of grace.

REFLECT
Reflect on God's desire for graceful words.

ACT
Pick a person and speak kind words of blessings to them.

YIELD
Meditate on the scriptures below.

SUPPORTING SCRIPTURES

Colossians 4:6 – Let your speech always be with grace, seasoned with salt, that you may know how you ought to answer each one.

Proverbs 18:20-21 – A man's belly shall be satisfied with the fruit of his mouth; and with the increase of his lips shall he be filled. Death and life are in the power of the tongue, and those who love it will eat its fruits.

Ephesians 4:29 – Let no corrupt communication proceed out of your mouth, but that which is good to the use of edifying, that it may minister grace unto the hearers.

Day 7
LEADERSHIP

Imagine what this world would look like today if God's concept of leadership were taught from the moment we were born. The idea that we are all created in the similitude of God and that divine call to stand in everything He created us to be would be the posture of how we approached life. What if the men in your life were reminded daily from their birth until now that they were equipped by God to lead— lead at their schools, lead in their homes, lead in their careers, lead in their communities. Imagine the possibilities!

Your first day on the job usually consists of being trained in the most important details in order to function in the absence of a supervisor or boss. When God created Adam and Eve, His first charge to them was concerning leadership and productivity. Because God is the boss, He made sure that

Day 7

Adam and Eve knew their job description and assignments in order to function.

We pray earnestly for this because we know that there are consequences to operating under poor leadership. We want and desperately need men who are willing to lead by way of God's divine design and we know that this type of leadership ordained by the LORD is what He desires.

The mere suggestion that a man should be fit to lead his household sends shock waves through the consciousness of many. Sometimes it can be intimidating to know that God has placed man as the head of woman because we interpret this with both a flawed and carnal perspective of leadership and submission. The wife's submission to her husband is a willful response as a result of his godly leadership and her submission does not suggest that she is inferior or subservient. When we follow God's plan for relationships being equally yoked, we are not overly grieved with this idea.

A man's call to lead does not suggest that he should be controlling and domineering, but it does mean that he should stand firmly planted within his role as chief steward and watchman over his family. Nothing soothes the heart of a woman more than knowing her heart is connected to a man who is unashamed to lovingly lead her, cover her, protect her, secure her, cherish her, and honor her worth.

PRAYER

Father God, I pray that You would call forth the leadership You've place on the life of _____. LORD, raise _____ up to be a strong and effective leader in life. God, Your Word says in Psalm 37:5 that if we commit our way to the Lord and trust in him, He will act. LORD, show Yourself mighty as _____ commits his way to You.

Father, I ask You to give him courage to assume his responsibilities as a leader whether in his home, at school, or among his peers. LORD, teach _____ that leadership is a call to service. Holy Spirit equip _____ with everything he needs to properly manage what has been entrusted to him. LORD, surround _____ with other Godly leaders who will help point the way to Your integrity. LORD, let his leadership reflect Your love and precepts as he humbly submits to the man that You have called him to be. In Jesus' name. Amen.

PRAYER REQUESTS/PRAISE REPORTS

_____

_____

_____

_____

Day 7

ACTION PLAN

PRAISE
Praise God for being the LORD of your life.

REFLECT
Reflect on the role(s) you have as a leader.

ACT
Take a moment to encourage a leader.

YIELD
Meditate on the scriptures below.

SUPPORTING SCRIPTURES

Psalm 37:5 – Commit your way to the LORD; trust in him and he will do this:

John 3:30 – He must increase, but I must decrease.

Matthew 20:26 – It is not this way among you, but whoever wishes to become great among you shall be your servant,

Day 8
PEACE

We often underestimate the value of peace until we don't have it. There are many men, both young and seasoned, who are not at a place of peace in their minds. Peace is what they need to reconcile the details of life to stand in their God-given positions. We pray that the men in our lives will understand that God Himself is not the creator of disorder and confusion, but He always has the power to sustain us in perfect peace - even in the midst of utter chaos.

Today we are seeking God for His peace to be upon his dear ones. We often ask God for things but many times we are so far away and disconnected from receiving what God provides because we have no peace. We often pray for peace, but do we really have the faith to believe that God will give it? Peace is a decision to rest in what God allows. When we pray, we pray His will and His Word concerning the matter

Day 8

and our expectancy of what we pray for is predicated upon whether our hearts and our minds are in agreement with God's Sovereignty—whatever He allows. When we are led by the Spirit of God, we yield to what He has promised despite what we see with our eyes or feel. You will maintain the peace of God when you get your mind right and keep it upon Him.

Cease not to give thanks for you, making mention of you in my prayers;
Ephesians 1:16

PRAYER

Holy Spirit, thank You for being the giver of true peace. LORD, let Your peace rule the heart of _____. LORD, guard his mind and give him the divine comfort in times of distress. Father, always give _____ calm delight in You. Help _____ to be mindful to pursue peace and walk in peace with others. LORD, Your Word declares if we keep our minds upon You, we would be kept in Your perfect peace. LORD, set an atmosphere of peace all around _____. Help _____ to keep his mind on You for the peace that only You can give. In Jesus' name. Amen.

PRAYER REQUESTS/PRAISE REPORTS

_____
_____
_____
_____
_____
_____
_____
_____

Day 8

ACTION PLAN

PRAISE
Praise God for the Prince of Peace.

REFLECT
Reflect on the power of peace at work in your life.

ACT
Listen to one of your favorite songs about peace.

YIELD
Meditate on the scriptures below.

SUPPORTING SCRIPTURES

Psalm 34:14 – Turn from evil and do good; seek peace and pursue it.

Philippians 4:7 – And the peace of God, which transcends all understanding, will guard your hearts and your minds in Christ Jesus.

Romans 15:13 – May the God of hope fill you with all joy and peace as you trust in him, so that you may overflow with hope by the power of the Holy Spirit.

Day 9
INTIMACY & SEXUAL PURITY

We live in a wicked and perverse world. There are tons of unholy influences which make many believe that sexual immorality is inevitable. So how do I say this...The devil IS a LIAR!!! We do not have to buy into this hyper-sensual sexualization of such an evil cultural conscience. Many are inundated with media images, secular music, entertainment, performers, fashion industries and the likes, with clearly defined ulterior motives. But because Satan is so cunning and divisive, we eat of the lies and become desensitized to the blatancy of sin itself.

God is the creator of sexuality and intimacy, and we have a responsibility to uphold the beauty of what He has given. Just how sinister it is that the enemy would try and turn a gift into a weapon through deceptive tactics. Let us pray and

Day 9

believe God to give the men in our lives a healthy and holy perspective regarding sex and intimacy.

Rejoicing in hope; patient in tribulation; continuing instant in prayer;
Romans 12:12

PRAYER

Father, I thank You for creating us with pleasures to enjoy according to Your will. I lift _____ before Your throne of grace that You would lead him to exercise control over his flesh. LORD, teach _____ that sex and intimacy are both beautiful gifts from You. LORD, sanctify his eyes that he may resist lust, self-gratification, sexual temptation, and any form of sexual immorality. Should temptations come, provide a way of escape so that he will be a man of honour. Holy Spirit, purge his mind of delusions, his heart of perversions, guard his eyes, and bless him to have complete satisfaction in the intimacy of his marital relationship alone. In Jesus' name. Amen.

PRAYER REQUESTS/PRAISE REPORTS

_____

_____

_____

_____

_____

_____

_____

Day 9

ACTION PLAN

PRAISE
Praise God for giving you a clean heart.

REFLECT
Reflect on the importance of understanding sex and intimacy as God designed.

ACT
Ask God to reveal any compromising areas in your life.

YIELD
Meditate on the scriptures below.

SUPPORTING SCRIPTURES

1 Corinthians 6:18 – Flee from sexual immorality. Every other sin a person commits is outside the body, but the sexually immoral person sins against his own body

Galatians 5:16 – But I say, walk by the Spirit, and you will not gratify the desires of the flesh

1 Corinthians 10:13 – There hath no temptation taken you but such as is common to man: but God is faithful, who will not suffer you to be tempted above that ye are able; but will with the temptation also make a way to escape, that ye may be able to bear it.

Day 10
HABITS

Habits are learned or assumed behaviours that become powerful forces in your life. They can be a virtue or a vice, and that depends upon whether they are building you up or tearing you down. We are products of the things we repeatedly do, say, or experience. Addictions, bad habits, vices, ungodly affiliations, and the likes are diametrically opposed to the Spirit of God. When we willingly allow ourselves to be connected to these things, we grieve the Holy Spirit. Little do we know that these entanglements can be just as deadly as sleeping with the enemy himself. Thank God for Jesus who has made the way for us to be overcomers because He Himself overcame the world and every work of the enemy. If you or someone you know is battling in their flesh or in their spirit, just know that through Jesus Christ you can overcome.

Day 10

PRAYER

Father, I thank You for Your delivering power. Your Word declares that whoever You set free will be free indeed. Send Your deliverance to _____ for his freedom. Release _____ from any bad habits, vices, substances, activities, affiliations or associations that conflict with Your plan for his life. Father, release _____ from the yoke of bondage and lead _____ in the path of righteousness for Your name's sake. Show _____ how to develop healthy habits for Godly living and surround him with everything he needs to overcome. LORD, illuminate his path as he seeks the way which leads to righteousness in You. Fill every void with Your goodness. In Jesus' name. Amen.

PRAYER REQUESTS/PRAISE REPORTS

_____
_____
_____
_____
_____
_____
_____
_____

ACTION PLAN

PRAISE — Praise God for His overcoming power.

REFLECT — Reflect on a time of deliverance in your life.

ACT — Share a testimony of deliverance with someone.

YIELD — Meditate on the scriptures below.

SUPPORTING SCRIPTURES

1 John 3:4 – Everyone who makes a practice of sinning also practices lawlessness; sin is lawlessness

Galatians 5:1 – Stand fast therefore in the liberty wherewith Christ hath made us free, and be not entangled again with the yoke of bondage

1 Corinthians 6:19-20 – Do you not know that your bodies are temples of the Holy Spirit, who is in you, whom you have received from God? You are not your own; you were bought at a price. Therefore, honor God with your bodies.

Day 10

Day 11
COMMITMENT

It takes nothing these days for someone to disconnect from something they once deemed important. That goes for anything from a job to a friend, and if you are connected to social media, you've witnessed the way people can "cut you off" - never to be spoken to or addressed again. The selfish nature of our flesh can lead us to cut things off that were never meant to be severed. If we allow it, the flesh will dictate to us in ways that will cost us dearly. It takes commitment to manage a career. In one area or another, life takes a heart of commitment.

Let us speak directly to marriages and relationships since this is a hot topic for many. It takes commitment to keep the flesh in line. It takes commitment to enter a relationship with a significant other. The same commitment, energy, and devotion we give in our courtships will be required to maintain

Day 11

our marriages and then some. Just because you finally got that ring and paper, you cannot afford to stop courting your mate. If you stop courting, then something or someone will compete for your position because you neglected to build upon what you started. Deferred maintenance in marriage can leave your relationship dilapidated and beyond repair if you are not careful and prayerful. If it was worth the start for the both of you then make it worth the finish.

But the end of all things is at hand: be ye therefore sober, and watch unto prayer. 1 Peter 4:7

PRAYER

Father, You are our example of true commitment, as Your Word promises that You will never leave us nor forsake us. God, I lift _____ before Your throne of grace. LORD, show _____ how to be fully committed to his faith, his vision, his wife/relationship, his family, and his good deeds. LORD, give _____ a determined heart to hold fast to his commitments and vows before You. Guide _____ in the path of righteous living by Your Spirit. LORD, teach _____ how to love, support, protect, provide, respect, and esteem his wife and family out of a sincere heart. In Jesus' name. Amen.

PRAYER REQUESTS/PRAISE REPORTS

_____

_____

_____

_____

_____

_____

_____

_____

_____

Day 11

ACTION PLAN

PRAISE
Praise God for being faithful to what He has promised.

REFLECT
Reflect on importance of honoring commitments.

ACT
Prayerfully reconsider any commitments where you may have been slack.

YIELD
Meditate on the scriptures below.

SUPPORTING SCRIPTURES

Proverbs 16:3 – Commit thy works unto the LORD, and thy thoughts shall be established.

1 Timothy 5:8 – But if anyone does not provide for his relatives, and especially for members of his household, he has denied the faith and is worse than an unbeliever.

Proverbs 20:6-7 – Many a man claims to have unfailing love, but a faithful man who can find? The righteous man leads a blameless life; blessed are his children after him.

Day 12
ATTITUDE

Our attitude is the way we act, think, and express our feelings. Our attitude also paints a picture of our perspectives, whether positive or negative. There could be a room filled with smiling faces, but one encounter from a person with a negative attitude can change the atmosphere of the entire room.

We have all heard the scenario of two people applying for the same position, but the one with the bad attitude in the interview is usually the one who loses out. God's Word tells us in Philippians 2:5 that our attitude should be the same as that of Christ Jesus. There is no example of Jesus displaying a bad attitude. We always find Jesus leading by positive examples and we always see His perspective from a place of truth. As we transform our mindset to the ways of Christ our

Day 12

thoughts and our feelings will align themselves to a more Christ-like attitude.

As we intercede for the men in our lives, let us prayerfully consider our own attitudes.

Pray without ceasing. 1 Thessalonians 5:17

PRAYER

Father God, I come to You on behalf of _____. LORD, Your Word sets the standard for how we should live life. God, I pray that _____ will take on an attitude that looks like You. LORD, I thank You for the transforming power of Your Word at work in _____. You said in Your Word that we should let the mind of Christ be in us. LORD, help _____ to think on good things and guide _____ as he expresses his thoughts and ideas in a beneficial way. Teach _____ to demonstrate Your grace through an attitude that reflects Your image. LORD, touch his heart and fill it with Your goodness. In Jesus' name. Amen.

PRAYER REQUESTS/PRAISE REPORTS

_____

_____

_____

_____

_____

_____

_____

Day 12

ACTION PLAN

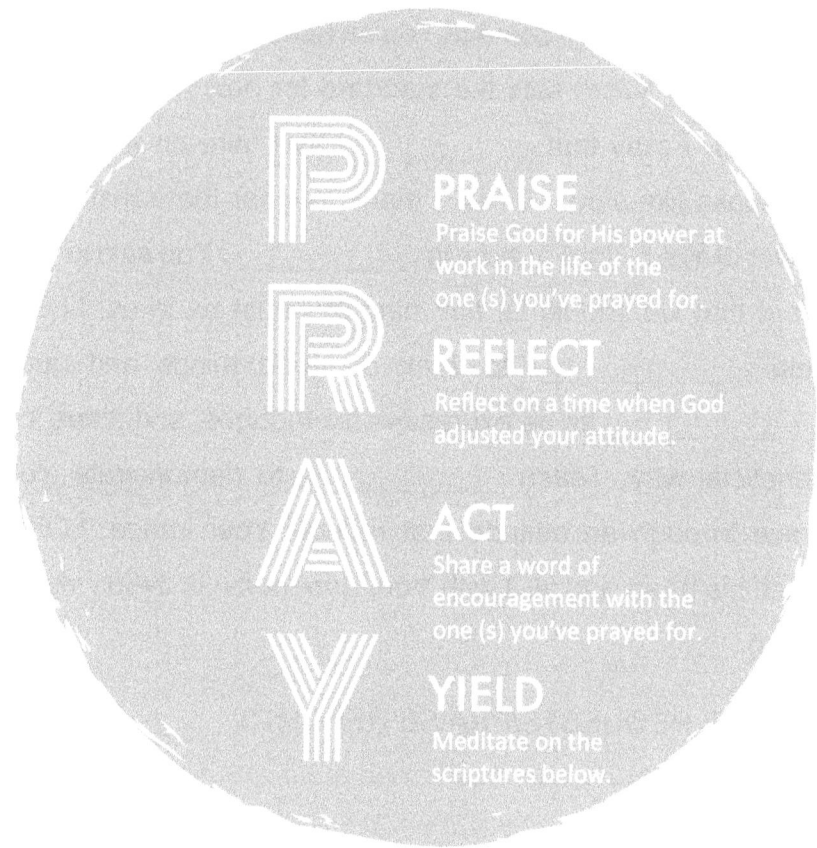

PRAISE — Praise God for His power at work in the life of the one(s) you've prayed for.

REFLECT — Reflect on a time when God adjusted your attitude.

ACT — Share a word of encouragement with the one(s) you've prayed for.

YIELD — Meditate on the scriptures below.

SUPPORTING SCRIPTURES

Philippians 2:14 – Do all things without murmurings and disputings:

Colossians 3:23 – And whatsoever ye do, do [it] heartily, as to the Lord, and not unto men;

Proverbs 17:22 – A merry heart doeth good [like] a medicine: but a broken spirit drieth the bones.

Day 13
STEWARDSHIP

The first thing that comes to mind when you think of stewardship is usually related to money. Believe me, it is so much more than money.

When God gave dominion to Adam and Eve in the garden, He appointed them to be managers (stewards) of the earth and its contents, but with the understanding that everything belonged to God regardless. They (Adam and Eve) had the responsibility of overseeing the operations of creation as well as having the luxury of indulging in the rich benefits of what was provided. The same responsibility has been passed on to all of us, but the earth's contents have transformed over time. We do not have to deal with lions, tigers and bears so much because we now have stocks, portfolios, businesses, ministries, property, careers, families, health, relationships, positions, possessions and yes...money. And the same God who owned the earth and its contents in the beginning is the

Day 13

same God who still owns it today. He has not given us a pass to be reckless in our management of the world and its contents. Instead, He charges us to be wise overseers of all that has been given to us knowing that He is the one who has given us the ability to get all that we have.

We are nothing without Him. Even in our nakedness and shame we are still nothing without Him. He loves us dearly and He values us more than we could ever imagine. So, when we say that we are nothing without Him we understand that we are partakers of His grace despite our shortcomings and our daily failures. So, the least we can do is honor Him with what already belongs to Him, which is everything; and we should be mindful to consult Him when dealing with His stuff. This should make it easier to love and easier to care and easier to give. You name it—He owns it. So yeah, that money thing is just a slice of stewardship.

PRAYER

Father, I thank You for being Sovereign God over everything. I lift _____ before Your throne. I pray that You would bless _____ to be a faithful steward over all that You have entrusted to him. Father, help _____ to be a wise manager of his time, talents, and treasures. Holy Spirit, help _____ to balance his faith, family, career, and priorities in a manner that pleases You. LORD, help _____ to be faithful in giving, wise in financial matters, and diligent in business. Help _____ to understand that You are the giver of every good and perfect gift. In Jesus' name. Amen.

PRAYER REQUESTS/PRAISE REPORTS

_____

_____

_____

_____

_____

_____

_____

_____

Day 13

ACTION PLAN

PRAISE
Praise God for teaching good stewardship to the one(s) you've prayed for.

REFLECT
Reflect on a time when you had to learn proper stewardship.

ACT
Think of an area of personal stewardship in need of help and adjust accordingly.

YIELD
Meditate on the scriptures below.

SUPPORTING SCRIPTURES

1 Corinthians 4:2 – Moreover it is required in stewards, that a man be found faithful.

1 Chronicles 29:11-12 – Everything in the heavens and earth is yours, O Lord, and this is your kingdom. We adore you as being in control of everything. Riches and honor come from you alone, and you are the Ruler of all mankind; your hand controls power and might and it is at your discretion that men are made great and given strength.

Matthew 6:21 – For where your treasure is, there your heart will be also

Day 14
HEALTH & PROSPERITY

God's desire for us is that we are whole and complete in every area of our lives. Paul said in 3 John 1:2 that it was his hope that they would be well and enjoy good health, even as their souls were doing well. That health and wellbeing included the total man--spiritually, physically, and mentally. I mean we are talking the soul, the body, the socio-emotional health and all the components which make up the whole of man. We earnestly pray for God's best for these men, but I want to bring balance to what we are praying for.

In the Kingdom of God there are countless promises and benefits to those who have made a conscious decision to accept Christ and live a life pleasing to Him by way of salvation. This position in Christ places us in covenant with God and when we honor this covenant by way of love and obedience to His word, He is obligated to us because of His

Day 14

Word. It is our position and posture to pray the prayer of faith and believe for God's best for our lives and understand that God is Sovereign. Sometimes in our finite understanding we feel that God's best for us means our own idea of a perfect world with the perfect family all snuggled in the perfect house with perfect careers and perfect smiles on those perfect faces every day (an exaggeration, no doubt). We can often seek our own perfection, but unknowingly dismiss God's perfection.

We live in a tainted world with tainted foods, dangerous chemicals/processes, sickness/diseases, and a whole other world of unknown dangers brought on by the wickedness in high places which makes our humanity vulnerable. But even considering all those things we are compelled to seek God for His best for us despite the things which pose a threat to our quality of life. The beauty is knowing that God says that in our frailty His strength is perfected in us so that in the event that we are faced with challenges whether spiritually, physically, or mentally we can be assured that He will equip us with what we need to prosper and be in health even as our souls prosper. Does God still heal today? YES! Does God still deliver today? YES! YES! Does God still regulate our mental faculties? YES! YES! and AMEN!!! But know that in this life there are many issues, BUT... Jesus says in John 16:33 to be encouraged because He has overcome the world!!! There may be some who we are praying for who need healing and we believe God for this, EMPHATICALLY! We also trust that God's grace is sufficient and available to all who need it and through His abundant grace and mercy we can walk in the perfection of His amazing strength and prosper in Him.

And all things, whatsoever ye shall ask in prayer, believing, ye shall receive. Matthew 21:22

Day 14

PRAYER

Father God, I seek Your face for the health and prosperity of _____. I believe that You have a hopeful future for _____. LORD, I pray that You would bless _____ to be prosperous and healthy in spirit, body, heart, and soul. Father God, anoint his spirit to be strong in Your mighty power. Anoint his mind to be sound and stable. Anoint his body to be made completely whole in You. LORD, Your Word says that if we seek wisdom and shun evil, we will have health and nourishment to our bodies. According to Your Word, bring health and nourishment to _____ as he follows Your precepts. LORD, let Your teachings be in his heart for long life, peace, and prosperity. Holy Spirit, grace _____ with all sufficiency according to Your Holy will. In Jesus' name. Amen.

PRAYER REQUESTS/PRAISE REPORTS

_____
_____
_____
_____
_____
_____

ACTION PLAN

PRAISE
Praise God for providing healing and prosperity for the one (s) you've prayed for.

REFLECT
Reflect on God's hand of healing and prosperity in your life.

ACT
Share a scripture of healing with someone in need.

YIELD
Meditate on the scriptures below.

SUPPORTING SCRIPTURES

Numbers 6:24-26 –The LORD bless you and keep you; the LORD make his face shine on you and be gracious to you; the LORD turn his face toward you and give you peace.'"

3 John 1:2 – Dear friend, I pray that you may enjoy good health and that all may go well with you, even as your soul is getting along well.

Isaiah 53:5 – But he was wounded for our transgressions, he was bruised for our iniquities: the chastisement of our peace was upon him; and with his stripes we are healed

Day 14

Day 15
HOLY CONVICTION

We live in perhaps one of the most pressure-driven societies of all times. We often face the pressure to achieve goals or the pressure to obtain status as a means of feeling accomplished and daily we are fueled with a sort of manic overdrive to compete with others and/or defend ourselves from others. And moreover, is the constant desensitizing of our moral consciousness. For every day we find ourselves laughing at distasteful jokes or becoming glued to the latest steamy novel featuring the glorification of ungodliness all the while reading it, it's making you desire the very defiled thing that God has delivered you from.

We demote ourselves another level into the pit of compromise by giving our stamp of approval to things which are designed to rot us to our very core. What a blatant attack on our convictions, but we just cannot seem to acknowledge

Day 15

the threat because in some way we act as if we are INVINCIBLE CHRISTIANS you know.

Today, our men are literally under fire. And often our men are confronted with very difficult decisions which challenge their character and convictions. So many are forced into a corner having to make a choice between what is right and what is convenient. They need courage under fire to draw the line between what pleases man and what pleases God. Will they have the strength to resist when the fellas are urging them to do something foolish? Will they be able to stand up and man up when the feeling of compromise feels so convenient?

We pray that God would raise up courageous men who are bold and unashamed. We pray that men will assume the call to righteousness daily and not just when righteousness is easy. The enemy's tactics are subtle, but God has provided a way of escape for all who will receive it. We are in a spiritual battle and not merely in competition with anyone—not even ourselves. We are praying that men would be led by God and receive His strength in the presence of their weakness. Be strong and do it.

PRAYER

Father, I honor You as being God of Righteousness. Holy Spirit, I ask You to lead _____ in the path of righteousness and holy conviction. Father, lead _____ to have a heart of compassion and mercy and give him courage to stand for what is right. Father God, You said in Your Word that we should seek justice, love mercy, and humbly walk with You. LORD, as _____ walks with You, let Your Spirit be the guide to his moral compass. Remove the seeds of immorality and apathy and replace them with seeds of righteousness. LORD, I ask you to bring conviction to _____ and bless him for doing what is right in Your sight. In Jesus' name. Amen.

PRAYER REQUESTS/PRAISE REPORTS

_____

_____

_____

_____

_____

_____

_____

Day 15

ACTION PLAN

PRAISE
Praise God for His truth in Christ Jesus.

REFLECT
Reflect on the Holy Spirit and His truth at work in your life.

ACT
Take an open stance for a cause you support.

YIELD
Meditate on the scriptures below.

SUPPORTING SCRIPTURES

2 Corinthians 4:8-9 – We are pressed on every side by troubles, but we are not crushed. We are perplexed, but not driven to despair. We are hunted down, but never abandoned by God. We get knocked down, but we are not destroyed.

Galatians 6:9 – So let's not get tired of doing what is good. At just the right time we will reap a harvest of blessing if we don't give up.

Joshua 1:9 – This is my command—be strong and courageous! Do not be afraid or discouraged. For the Lord your God is with you wherever you go."

Day 16
HUMILITY

It is an easy thing to be prideful these days. With all the self-help books and motivational messages we see, many of them send mixed signals. While motivation should be used to encourage us and affirm our strengths, sometimes we find ourselves hyped to levels of pride where we begin to see ourselves as dominators over others, or we begin to feel a sense of superiority. We are powerful, but our power needs balance.

One of the most powerful concentrations of energy we encounter daily is electricity. It takes 1200 watts of electricity to power a house lamp. In comparison, it takes 11 billion watts of electricity per day to power the city of New York, which is about the same measure of electricity in a lightning bolt!! Imagine all that energy being unleashed in any city without a balance of power. Thank God for safe power lines and

Day 16

conduits to balance all that energy. When a person's ego is unchecked, it can unleash the potential for prideful destruction, but when humility comes, that same power is a benefit.

The bible tells us in Psalm 139:14 that "we are fearfully and wonderfully made" by God, but it also tells us in Romans 12:3 that "we should not think of ourselves more highly than we should." One of the fruits of the Spirit is meekness, but many forget that meekness is not weakness. We can be everything that God has purposed us to be, but humility is a position of honor which exalts God above self. Let us pray God's humility to be evident in the lives of the men we hold dear.

Hear my prayer, oh LORD. Psalm 142:1

PRAYER

Father, I thank You for creating _____ in Your likeness. LORD, give _____ the will to walk in humility. Holy Spirit, I pray that You would guide _____ to temper his ego so that his attitude will not be overtaken in pride. Father, thank You for showing _____ the benefits of patience at work. You said in Your Word that those who humble themselves will be exalted by You in due time. Help _____ to remain humble and aware of the goodness that You have invested in him. LORD, give_____ a healthy perspective of self. In Jesus' name. Amen.

PRAYER REQUESTS/PRAISE REPORTS

_____

_____

_____

_____

_____

_____

_____

_____

Day 16

ACTION PLAN

PRAISE — Praise God for providing a heart of humility for the one(s) you've prayed for.

REFLECT — Reflect on a time when you resisted pride.

ACT — Ask God to reveal and adjust any areas in your life where pride may linger.

YIELD — Meditate on the scriptures below.

SUPPORTING SCRIPTURES

1 Peter 5:6 – Humble yourselves therefore under the mighty hand of God, that he may exalt you in due time:

Romans 12:3 – For I say, through the grace given unto me, to every man that is among you, not to think [of himself] more highly than he ought to think; but to think soberly, according as God hath dealt to every man the measure of faith.

1 Peter 5:5 – Likewise, ye younger, submit yourselves unto the elder. Yea, all [of you] be subject one to another, and be clothed with humility: for God resisteth the proud, and giveth grace to the humble.

Day 17
SELF ESTEEM

What good is dirt? I am talking about the icky stuff on the bottom of your shoe after a jog through the park. It is the worthless gunk underneath the nails that we wash frequently. But what if I told you that dirt was like gold. Without dirt we would not have soil to grow food. Without dirt, there would be no foundation to build upon. What is worthless in the eyes of some can be priceless to others. God feels the same way about His creation. Some have the tendency to attach a value to a person based upon their personal value system, but not realizing that God has already ascribed value to every single one of His children. The value of His creation is so great that He sent His Son to pay the ultimate immeasurable price just to save us.

It is an easy thing to rip someone apart, but it takes real effort to build and encourage. For every time someone has

Day 17

spoken negatively towards a child to suggest that they were incapable of learning, God says, "Not so!" For every derogatory word spoken over the life of a young man, God says, "Not so!" For every attempt to sabotage the self-worth of a husband or a father, God says, "Not so!" It is our prayer that the men in our lives will see themselves as Christ sees them. As we intercede for them, we pray that God will give them constant reminders of the greatness that lies within.

These all continued with one accord in prayer and supplication, Acts 1:14

PRAYER

Father, I thank You for creating _____ for Your glory. I pray that You would give _____ a sense of personal esteem and worth which comes from You. LORD, Your Word declares that our sufficiency lies within You. I plead the covenant blood of Jesus over every negative thing that seeks to diminish his worth. Holy Spirit, I ask You to teach _____ how to love and respect himself as a product of Your workmanship. Help _____ to know that his life is precious in Your sight and through Christ, he has unconditional love from You. In Jesus' name. Amen.

PRAYER REQUESTS/PRAISE REPORTS

_____

_____

_____

_____

_____

_____

_____

_____

_____

Day 17

ACTION PLAN

PRAISE — Praise God for being the example of faithfulness.

REFLECT — Reflect on being created in the similitude of Christ Jesus.

ACT — Share your favorite scripture with someone.

YIELD — Meditate on the scriptures below.

SUPPORTING SCRIPTURES

1 Peter 2:9 – But you are a chosen generation, a royal priesthood, a holy nation, His own special people, that you may proclaim the praises of Him who called you out of darkness into His marvelous light

Genesis 1:27 – So God created man in his [own] image, in the image of God created he him; male and female created he them

Ephesians 2:10 – For we are His workmanship, created in Christ Jesus for good works, which God prepared beforehand that we should walk in them.

Day 18
FORGIVENESS

In the flesh, it feels natural and justifiable to hold grudges against anyone who causes us hurt or harm. When we know that someone took aim at our hearts in any way to harm us, our flesh seeks instant vindication and when vindication doesn't come, we are willing to hold on to a payback agenda for as long as it takes, not realizing that unforgiveness is often a more potent venom to ourselves than to others. God tells us that true vengeance belongs to Him, and we will all give an answer for the deeds we have done in our flesh. But even more powerful than God's vengeance is His great mercy, and just as He has shown mercy towards us, we should be willing to show mercy in our acts of forgiveness.

God's Word tells us in Ephesians 4:32 that we should "[forgive] others just as Christ forgives us." Today we pray that God will lead hearts to forgiveness.

Day 18

PRAYER

Father God, I praise You for Your great mercies. I thank You that Your hand rests upon _____. Your Word declares that Your mercies are renewed each morning. Thank You for being merciful to _____. LORD, bring healing and deliverance from all seeds of unforgiveness. LORD, restore his heart and mind to a place of forgiveness so that he can be at peace within and with others. I plead the covenant blood of Jesus against bitterness, rage, anger, and guile. Holy Spirit, touch his heart and give him a holy conviction towards reconciliation. Set _____ free from past hurts and disappointments and release Your joy and freedom. Give _____ the freedom to release the past and embrace Your hope and future for him. In Jesus' name. Amen.

PRAYER REQUESTS/PRAISE REPORTS

_____

_____

_____

_____

_____

_____

ACTION PLAN

PRAISE — Praise God for providing forgiveness to the one (s) you've prayed for.

REFLECT — Reflect on what forgiveness has meant to you.

ACT — Ask God to reveal repair any areas of unforgiveness in you.

YIELD — Meditate on the scriptures below.

SUPPORTING SCRIPTURES

James 5:16 – Confess your faults one to another, and pray one for another, that ye may be healed. The effectual fervent prayer of a righteous man availeth much.

Ephesians 4:32 – And be ye kind one to another, tenderhearted, forgiving one another, even as God for Christ's sake hath forgiven you.

Matthew 6:14 – For if ye forgive men their trespasses, your heavenly Father will also forgive you.

Day 18

Day 19
FAITHFULNESS

One of the most grievous processes for me to observe is that of a young woman's unrelenting hopes of having a man transition into a committed relationship with her after he has pledged permanency, and by committed relationship, I mean marriage. I mean, we're talking two seemingly mature adults with the time and ability to collect the data necessary to come to a reasonable conclusion about their future together...that's why we have dating so that we can collect data. Sometimes it can be 5 or maybe even 10 years' worth of an investment of time, energy and sacrifices and the only return yielded is a laundry list of reasons why he is just not ready to enter covenant. Fear of Commitment is the new catch phrase for guys who avoid making a firm decision. Somehow, he manages to tiptoe around the details of responsibility, yet he still appears sincere—just enough to keep her hoping.

Day 19

Sometimes scenarios like this come from a place of uncertainty, but often they come from a more lackluster place of cowardice. Some men are not willing to take a stand on either side of the line of moral fortitude and since they're afforded the opportunity to extend their trial offer with all of the benefits for as long as they can keep up the ruse then they have no real urging to do anything different. I suppose that's where the friends with benefits idea comes from. And we used to be able to say that this applies only to the young and foolish, but that age bracket is broadening by the day.

The bible says in James 5:12, "But above all, my brothers, do not swear, either by heaven or by earth or by any other oath, but let your "yes" be yes and your "no" be no, so that you may not fall under condemnation." Some men make vain promises to misguided hearts saying things like, "I'm going to marry you, but I've got to work on some stuff first" or "Girl, you know I'm not going anywhere" just to put an indefinite pin in it. And I'm not suggesting that a man jump into a marriage just for the sake of marriage, but I am saying that a Godly man should consider what is required of him when he enters into a relationship and he should be forthcoming with his intentions in that relationship. And neither am I laying all the blame on men, but our focus is on men today. This same attitude in relationships translates to other areas of life. I would take time to explore the 'whys' but I'll save it for another time.

God takes vows and promises very seriously and he says that it is better for us to not make a promise at all rather than make a promise and then break it (Ecclesiastes 5). A man's ability to honor, appreciate and respect relationships speaks to his character and his willingness to be faithful to what he has promised. God delights in those who are faithful to what they have promised (Proverbs 12). Pray earnestly for men and their will to be faithful and committed and pray for their willingness to be forthcoming with their intentions.

Call unto me, and I will answer thee, and shew thee great and mighty things, which thou knowest not. Jeremiah 33:3

Day 19

PRAYER

Father God, I thank You for being the ultimate example of faithfulness. I lift _____ before Your throne. Father, create in _____ a clean heart and renew a right spirit within him. LORD, lead _____ to an uncompromising life of faithfulness to You, his family, and to his responsibilities and reward _____ for his faithfulness. LORD, Your Word tells us in 1 Corinthians 4:2 that faithfulness is a requirement for those who have been entrusted with something of value. I pray that _____ will honor his promises and be intentional with his commitments. I pray that _____ will be faithful to all that has been entrusted to him. In Jesus' name. Amen.

PRAYER REQUESTS/PRAISE REPORTS

_____
_____
_____
_____
_____
_____
_____

ACTION PLAN

PRAISE
Praise God for His great faithfulness.

REFLECT
Reflect on what faithfulness means to you.

ACT
Reaffirm your faithfulness to someone you value.

YIELD
Meditate on the scriptures below.

SUPPORTING SCRIPTURES

Proverbs 28:20 – A faithful man shall abound with blessings: but he that maketh haste to be rich shall not be innocent.

Hebrews 10:23 – Let us hold fast the profession of our faith without wavering; (for he is faithful that promised;)

Romans 10:9-11 – Let love be without hypocrisy. Abhor what is evil; cling to what is good. Be devoted to one another in brotherly love; give preference to one another in honor; not lagging behind in diligence, fervent in spirit, serving the Lord;

Day 19

Day 20
FAVOR

Have you ever received a check in the mail from an unexpected source? Or have you ever received an upgrade or free ticket to a play that you have always wanted to see, but they were always sold out? Perhaps you have encountered a seasoned church member or a loved one placing a sum of money in your hand unexpectedly with no obligation to repay (we used to call that a Holy Ghost Handshake in my day). How did it make you feel? Those are examples of receiving a level of unmerited graceful benefits that you did not deserve, but you received it anyway "just because." God gives His dear ones' moments of undeserved benefits at His discretion just because He is God. God will open doors of opportunity to His children just because. God will allow you to be the one promoted on a job when there is someone more qualified for the position. God will grant access

Day 20

to unmerited graceful benefits to you just because. When God's favor is upon you, He allows you to experience unmerited graceful benefits that you did not deserve to receive and He is never obligated to give, but He chooses to give it…just because. Today we pray for God's favor upon the men in our lives, that they will experience unmerited graceful benefits from the true and living God.

> But when ye pray, use not vain repetitions, as the heathen do: for they think that they shall be heard for their much speaking. Matthew 6:7

PRAYER

Abba Father, I acknowledge Your amazing love for Your children. I lift _____ before Your throne of grace. LORD, let Your hand of favor be upon _____. Your Word declares in Psalm 90:17 that You establish the works of the hands of those who have favor with You. God, I pray that You will give _____ unmerited graceful benefits daily. Holy Spirit, open doors for _____, make ways for _____, and provide for _____ in ways that are beyond what he deserves. Let there be no lack in his house as You establish his way. Bless _____ with favor with You and with man. In Jesus' name. Amen.

PRAYER REQUESTS/PRAISE REPORTS

_____

_____

_____

_____

_____

_____

_____

_____

Day 20

ACTION PLAN

PRAISE
Praise God for providing favor to the one (s) you've prayed for.

REFLECT
Reflect on a time where God's favor prevailed for you.

ACT
Ask God to give you one person to bless in any way He leads.

YIELD
Meditate on the scriptures below.

SUPPORTING SCRIPTURES

Psalm 90:17 – Let the favor of the Lord our God be upon us, and establish the work of our hands upon us; yes, establish the work of our hands!

Philippians 4:19 – And my God will supply every need of yours according to his riches in glory in Christ Jesus.

Ephesians 1:11 – In him we have obtained an inheritance, having been predestined according to the purpose of him who works all things according to the counsel of his will,

Day 21
ACCOUNTABILITY

Statistics show that nearly 60 million Americans are enrolled in a gym membership. And of those 60 million people, 80 percent of those memberships go unused. In comparison, Americans who incorporate a personal fitness trainer are more likely to remain consistent in a fitness routine. It all boils down to accountability. Accountability leans upon a moral commitment to personal responsibilities and it puts a support system in place for one's success. Just like the cheerleaders and the fans show up for the basketball team, that level of support is a driving force for the team's hunger to win. There is no feeling like knowing that someone has your back.

As we pray for the accountability of the men in our lives, we pray that God will provide a support system (both inwardly and outwardly) for the men in our lives, so that they will be held accountable.

Day 21

PRAYER

Father, I come to You in the name of Jesus on behalf of _____. I thank You for giving _____ strength to follow through with every task given to him. LORD, Your Word says in Romans 12:14 that we are all accountable to You. Holy Spirit, lead _____ to be accountable in his words, actions, attitude and responsibilities. Father God, surround _____ with encouragement through Your Word and from Godly counsel. LORD, give _____ an inward resolve to follow through with his commitments. LORD, show _____ the ways of Your righteousness. In Jesus' name. Amen.

PRAYER REQUESTS/PRAISE REPORTS

_____
_____
_____
_____
_____
_____
_____

ACTION PLAN

PRAISE
Praise God for providing strength to the one (s) you've prayed for.

REFLECT
Reflect on a time where you were held accountable.

ACT
Offer a word of support to encourage someone in need.

YIELD
Meditate on the scriptures below.

SUPPORTING SCRIPTURES

Proverbs 11:14 – Where no counsel is, the people fall: but in the multitude of counsellors there is safety.

1 Thessalonians 5:11 – Therefore encourage one another and build one another up, just as you are doing.

Matthew 12:36-37 – I tell you, on the day of judgment people will give account for every careless word they speak, for by your words you will be justified, and by your words you will be condemned."

Day 21

Day 22
COMPASSION

When you think of the way God has fashioned the kindness that shows up in humanity, you can't help but get a glimpse of the depth of God's own heart. Each story we see of a total stranger showing up in the nick of time to save a pedestrian from a burning vehicle, or an anonymous donor helping a family through financial ruin—these moments are reminders that people have the capacity to demonstrate God's heart to others.

In the ministry of Jesus, we see the ultimate example of compassion when He refuses to allow people to leave His presence in the same state they were when they first encountered Him. He was moved with compassion and He was compelled to make a difference. Today, our prayer is that God will impress His heart of compassion upon the men in our lives.

Day 22

PRAYER

God, I bless You because You are my God. I thank You that You have given _____ the capacity to show compassion to others as a selfless act of love. God, I thank You for giving _____ a genuine heart towards the things that touch Your heart. God, Your Word urges us to do for others as we would want them to do for us. Holy Spirit, plant _____ firmly into Your love and teach _____ how to demonstrate Your compassion to others. LORD, lead _____ to be kind, selfless, and forgiving. Father God, let _____ be an agent of change as Your ambassador. In Jesus' name. Amen.

PRAYER REQUESTS/PRAISE REPORTS

_____
_____
_____
_____
_____
_____
_____
_____

ACTION PLAN

PRAISE
Praise God for His unfailing compassion.

REFLECT
Reflect on a time when someone showed compassion towards you.

ACT
Ask God to show you ways to be more compassionate to others.

YIELD
Meditate on the scriptures below.

SUPPORTING SCRIPTURES

Colossians 3:12 – Put on then, as God's chosen ones, holy and beloved, compassionate hearts, kindness, humility, meekness, and patience,

Matthew 7:12 – In everything, therefore, [a]treat people the same way you want them to treat you, for this is the Law and the Prophets.

1 Peter 4:10 – As each has received a gift, use it to serve one another, as good stewards of God's varied grace:

Day 22

Day 23
JOY

Happiness is an experience we create, but joy comes from the LORD. God's desire for His dear ones' is the experience of happiness and joy, but we should realize that joy is a quality more consistent than happiness can provide. So, why do some men chase money, women, substances, and other temporal things more than they seek joy? Maybe it comes from a longing to please the flesh through tangible things. I think we often forget that happiness is conditional, and it only likes to hang around when conditions are just right. And once circumstances change, or the money is gone, or a relationship goes sour, happiness will try to make an exit. On the other hand, God's joy is the experience of overwhelming contentment from within and it is unconditional. Joy is God's way of giving us a continual refreshing of our inner being which fills our hearts and overtakes our emotions in a way that

Day 23

happiness can never fulfill. And when circumstances change, God's unconditional joy remains.

As we pray for the men in our lives, we petition God for a release of His divine joy for them. We pray that they will experience the fullness of a fruitful life with nothing missing and nothing lacking.

Let us therefore come boldly unto the throne of grace, that we may obtain mercy, and find grace to help in time of need. Hebrews 4:16

PRAYER

Father God, I thank You for blessing us with good things to enjoy. I lift _____ before You right now. LORD, fill his heart with joy and happiness. Holy Spirit, overtake _____ in Your presence, and let _____ experience the fulness of Your joy. LORD, when circumstances change, let _____ consider it pure joy as he places his trust in You. Bless _____ to enjoy the fruit of his labour and the joy of salvation in You. LORD, teach _____ to be content in all that You bless him to receive and experience. Fill _____ with shouts of joy and singing in honor of Your goodness. In Jesus' name. Amen.

PRAYER REQUESTS/PRAISE REPORTS

_____

_____

_____

_____

_____

_____

_____

_____

Day 23

ACTION PLAN

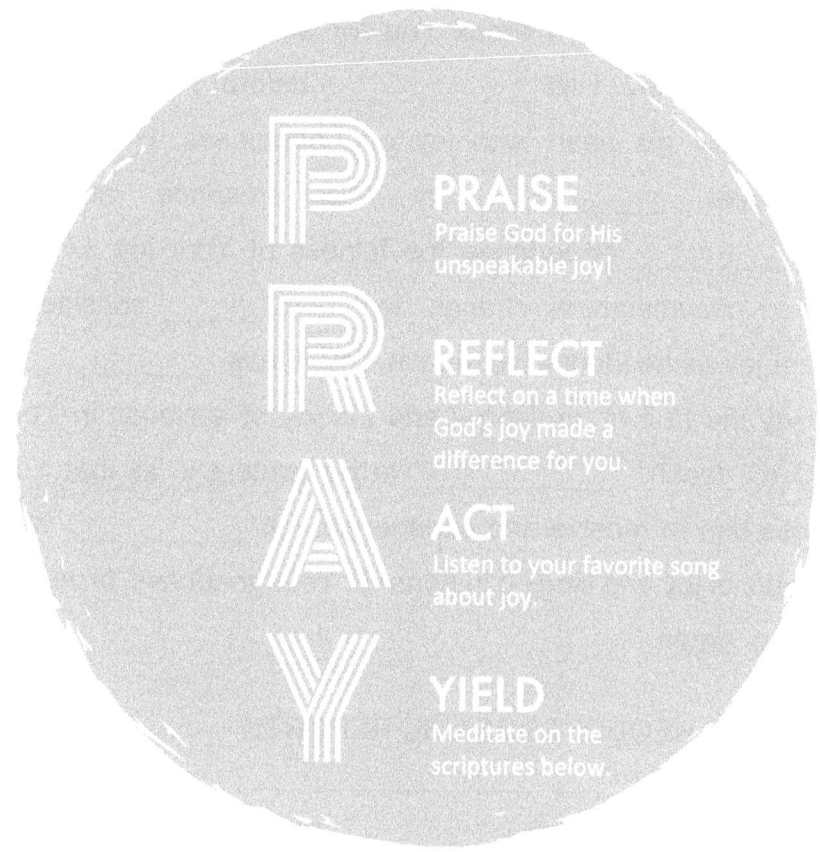

PRAISE — Praise God for His unspeakable joy!

REFLECT — Reflect on a time when God's joy made a difference for you.

ACT — Listen to your favorite song about joy.

YIELD — Meditate on the scriptures below.

SUPPORTING SCRIPTURES

Philippians 4:4 – Rejoice in the Lord always: and again I say, Rejoice.

James 1:2-3 – Consider it pure joy, my brothers, whenever you face trials of many kinds, because you know that the testing of your faith develops perseverance.

Psalm 30:5 – For his anger endureth but a moment; in his favour is life: weeping may endure for a night, but joy cometh in the morning.

Day 24
PROTECTION

The Word of God tells us in John 10:10 that the thief comes with the sole intent to steal, to kill, and to destroy. It does not matter who you are or where you are from, the enemy seeks to place a wedge between mankind and God, and he will use any accessible avenue to ensure his success. And there are enemies both seen and unseen which seek to hinder us, but in that same passage of John 10:10, Jesus said, "I am come that they might have life, and that they might have it more abundantly."

One can hardly get through a newspaper or a local newscast without hearing of devastation. It's not God's desire for us to walk in fear of what we see on social media or what we hear on the news, but we should fully rely on God to keep us and our loved ones covered under His divine protection.

Day 24

Just as we pray for our own protection, we pray for God to keep our loved ones safe.

As believers, we depend upon the mercies of God daily, and His love for us provides protection from the hand of the enemy. Just as Jesus gives us life, He also provides divine protection as the Good Shepherd who cares for His sheep. If animals have an innate sense to guard their young, how much more will the Good Shepherd guard those who put their trust in Him?

But let him ask in faith, nothing wavering. For he that wavereth is like a wave of the sea driven with the wind and tossed. James 1:6

PRAYER

Father God, I adore You as being the Sovereign LORD of my life. I thank You for being a shield and defense in times of need. LORD, cover _____. Stretch forth Your mighty hand of protection and keep _____ under Your covering. LORD. Your Word declares that Your name is a strong tower where the righteous run in and they are saved. Holy Spirit, be a sword and shield for _____. LORD, deliver _____ from the snare of the enemy and protect him from hurt, harm, and danger. I plead the covenant blood of Jesus against all demonic forces, evil plot or plans, and anything that seeks to harm _____. God, I thank You for upholding _____ with Your righteous hand. No weapon formed against _____ will succeed. In Jesus' name. Amen.

PRAYER REQUESTS/PRAISE REPORTS

_____

_____

_____

_____

_____

_____

Day 24

ACTION PLAN

PRAISE — Praise God for protecting the one (s) you've prayed for.

REFLECT — Reflect on a time when God's hand of protection covered you.

ACT — Share a scripture about God's protection with someone.

YIELD — Meditate on the scriptures below.

SUPPORTING SCRIPTURES

Isaiah 41:10 – Fear not, for I am with you; be not dismayed, for I am your God; I will strengthen you, I will help you, I will uphold you with my righteous right hand.

2 Thessalonians 3:3 – But the Lord is faithful. He will establish you and guard you against the evil one.

Isaiah 54:17 – No weapon that is fashioned against you shall succeed, and you shall confute every tongue that rises against you in judgment. This is the heritage of the servants of the Lord and their vindication from me, declares the Lord.

Day 25
FRIENDSHIPS & RELATIONSHIPS

Friendships and relationship can be so shallow these days. At any given moment, the person you thought would be in your life forever is subject to abandon you without notice. Knowing this, we should be careful when choosing who we connect with. Our friendships and relationships are critical elements of our environment and our environment impacts our thoughts, actions and decisions. Before we know it, the same attributes we once despised can take root in our own lives and become the attributes we embrace. But how many of us are careful with whom we connect? How many of us have carefully and prayerfully considered the value of true friendships? Our friendships and relationships are meant to build us and make us better and often we connect to people

Day 25

who do not encourage us to be better or to grow. We would rather have the quantity and not the quality of friendship. It's not that friendships and relationships are perfect, but the heart of true friendships and relationships should be based on an unselfish act of love.

Bless them that curse you, and pray for them which despitefully use you.

Luke 6:28

PRAYER

Gracious Father, You have been the consistent source of all I need. LORD. I come to You on behalf of _____. I pray that You will bless _____ with genuine friendships and healthy relationships with others. LORD, bless _____ with supportive friends who will be quick to listen, wise in Godly counsel, and who will enhance his walk with Christ. Your Word says in Proverbs 17:17 that a friend loves at all times. LORD, surround _____ with people who love him and care for him. Holy Spirit give _____ divine connections with people who love You and have his best interests at heart. LORD, bless _____ with true friendships that are committed to honoring You. LORD, reveal those who have impure intentions. In Jesus' name. Amen.

PRAYER REQUESTS/PRAISE REPORTS

_____

_____

_____

_____

_____

_____

Day 25

ACTION PLAN

PRAISE
Praise God for the gift of friendship.

REFLECT
Reflect on the blessing of friendship.

ACT
Reach out to a friend and thank them for their friendship.

YIELD
Meditate on the scriptures below.

SUPPORTING SCRIPTURES

Ecclesiastes 4:9-10 – Two are better than one, because they have a good reward for their toil. For if they fall, one will lift up his fellow. But woe to him who is alone when he falls and has not another to lift him up!

John 15:12-14 – This is my commandment, that you love one another as I have loved you. Greater love has no one than this, that someone lay down his life for his friends. You are my friends if you do what I command you.

Job 6:14 – He who withholds kindness from a friend forsakes the fear of the Almighty.

Day 26
PURPOSE & ABILITIES

It is reassuring to know that God has a purpose and plan for our lives. His Word tells us that He knew us before we were born, and He knows us by name. Of the countless people who have inhabited the earth, there has never been a duplicate set of fingerprints and we are all unique in our gifts and talents. Whether you are good at math or you have a knack for making people laugh, you have something of value to contribute to this world. Even after knowing all of this, many people struggle to figure out the reason for their existence—they want to know their purpose.

God's Word reminds us in Isaiah 43:7 that we have been created for His glory. So whatever it is you find yourself doing, make sure that it brings God glory. You know that you are walking in purpose when what you do brings honor to God.

Day 26

As we pray for the men in our lives, we pray for each gift, talent, skill, calling, and ability to reveal purpose unto the glory of God.

And at midnight Paul and Silas prayed, and sang praises unto God: and the prisoners heard them. Acts 16:25

PRAYER

Our Father, You are Creator of all things. I am grateful for every breath you have given. LORD, I lift _____ before You right now. Reveal Your purpose to him and teach him Your ways. God, You said in Your Word that we are Your workmanship, created in Christ Jesus unto good works, of which You ordained us to walk. LORD, lead _____ to walk in all that You have ordained for his life. LORD, remind _____ that You have created him with gifts, talents, skills, callings, and abilities which are meant to bring You glory. Holy Spirit, anoint _____ for true purpose in You. Bless _____ to work heartily as unto the LORD, and reassure _____ that You have created him with a hopeful future. In Jesus' name. Amen.

PRAYER REQUESTS/PRAISE REPORTS

_____

_____

_____

_____

_____

Day 26

ACTION PLAN

PRAISE
Praise God for giving a hope and future to the one(s) you've prayed for.

REFLECT
Reflect on the gifts and abilities you have.

ACT
Celebrate the gifts and abilities of someone you know.

YIELD
Meditate on the scriptures below.

SUPPORTING SCRIPTURES

Proverbs 22:29 - Seest thou a man diligent in his business? he shall stand before kings; he shall not stand before mean men.

Isaiah 42:7 – [Even] every one that is called by my name ; for I have created him for my glory, I have formed him ; yea, I have made him.

Philippians 4:13 – I can do all things through Christ which strengtheneth me.

Day 27
SPIRITUAL GROWTH

Corporate America capitalizes upon growth. There are countless multi-million-dollar businesses who depend upon growth in order to sell their goods and services. They depend upon your financial growth and resources so that they will make the largest profits possible. They depend upon the growth cycles, even the growth cycles of your lives to upsell the next size of jeans or to sell the next house. Not to mention, many companies profit as annual birthday celebrations have evolved over the last several years to spark a whole new concept of glam birthday parties and upscale celebrations. No one is knocking the idea of celebrating another year of blessing, but how many celebrations do we see taking place for our spiritual growth? How many corporations are featuring personal spiritual growth in their quarterly publications? It is a nice thought, but that would likely never happen. People have

Day 27

the tendency to be more in tuned with the benefits of natural growth than spiritual growth. Even so, God's Word asks in Mark 8:36, what does it profit a man if he should gain the whole world, yet forfeit his soul?

Our spiritual growth in Christ is more important than our natural growth. It is God's will for us to see progress in every area of life, but our spiritual growth is the lifeline of our connection to Him. If we lack growth in spirit, we lack development in the core of who we really are.

These all continued with one accord in prayer and supplication, with the women, and Mary the mother of Jesus, and with his brethren. Acts 1:14

PRAYER

Abba Father, You are the maker of heaven and earth. Thank You for creating _____ for Your divine purpose. I pray that You will give _____ a hunger and thirst for Your righteousness. LORD, nourish his spirit so that he will grow in the grace and knowledge of who You are. LORD, give _____ insight and revealed knowledge of Your Holy Word. Give _____ faith to believe Your Word and erase any form of doubt regarding Your truth. Father God, give _____ strength to daily put away the carnal nature in exchange for life in Your Spirit. Bless _____ with fellowship in Your Spirit and remove any hindrances to his spiritual maturity in Christ. In Jesus' name. Amen.

PRAYER REQUESTS/PRAISE REPORTS

_____

_____

_____

_____

_____

_____

Day 27

ACTION PLAN

SUPPORTING SCRIPTURES

Matthew 5:6 – Blessed are those who hunger and thirst for righteousness, for they will be filled.

1 Peter 3:18 – But grow in grace, and *in* the knowledge of our Lord and Saviour Jesus Christ. To him *be* glory both now and for ever. Amen.

Ephesians 5:1 – Be ye therefore followers of God, as dear children;

Day 28
HEART OF PRAYER & WORSHIP

Sometimes people become so complacent in life that nothing moves them to prayer— even when they are the ones who are in desperate need of divine intervention. In order for them to be moved to give reverence to God in worship, it takes something tragic to get them to that place. Even the nonbeliever will call out to God in times of distress.

As we ponder in scripture and pray God's Word over the men who have been placed in our lives, let us not wait until our foundation is shaken before we are moved to prayer. Seek the LORD now while He can be found and call unto Him while He is near. Prayer is always in order and it is our protocol in times of peace as well as turmoil. When we make prayer a daily application, we avoid the appearance of "pimpin" God for

Day 28

what we can get out of Him in our time of need only to abandon Him when He's given us what we wanted. Let us pray for constant communion in prayer and worship!

Be careful for nothing; but in everything by prayer and supplication with thanksgiving let your requests be made known unto God. Philippians 4:6

PRAYER

Holy One, I honour You as King of all kings and LORD over everything. I call upon Your Holy Name to manifest Yourself to _____ in a mighty way. Father God, lead and guide _____ to Your truth through daily communion. LORD, let _____ abide in You and Your Spirit abide in him. Touch _____ in his inner man and lead _____ to a lifestyle of worship and prayer. LORD, You said in Your Word that those who worship You must worship You in spirit and in truth. I pray that _____ will give You glory with the fruit of his lips, and through a heart of worship to You. Let the words of his mouth and the meditation of his heart be holy and acceptable in Your sight. Holy Spirit consume _____ with Your fire as he receives a deeper understanding of his covenant with You. Make _____ to know that he is uniquely chosen for the glory of God. In Jesus' name. Amen.

PRAYER REQUESTS/PRAISE REPORTS

_____

_____

_____

_____

_____

Day 28

ACTION PLAN

PRAISE
Praise God for being your Heavenly Father.

REFLECT
Reflect on the impact of prayer and worship in your life.

ACT
Listen to your favorite worship song.

YIELD
Meditate on the scriptures below.

SUPPORTING SCRIPTURES

John 4:24 – God is spirit, and those who worship him must worship in spirit and truth."

Psalm 29:2 – Ascribe to the Lord the glory due his name; worship the Lord in the splendor of holiness

Psalm 95:6 – Oh come, let us worship and bow down; let us kneel before the Lord, our Maker!

Day 29
GODLY MORALS & VALUES

Our values are the concepts whereby we measure the true worth, benefit, importance, usefulness or significance of something or someone. When our value system is flawed, we become capable of taking away the significance of something of worth. As a result of this value deficit, we are subject to poor judgment, and things that need our attention often become overlooked, neglected, abused, and abandoned—including our own selves. Our ability to determine right from wrong does not come from our own ability, but God is our only source of righteousness.

Throughout scripture, we receive a healthy perspective of how we should honor and respect others. Christ gives the ultimate example of Godly morals and values as He urges us to treat people the way we would want to be treated.

Day 29

PRAYER

Father God, I exalt You above all things. I bring _____ before You. You have given us Your Word for instruction and guidance, and I pray that Your Word will be revealed to _____. LORD, show _____ Your ways and teach_____ how to respect himself and others as Your creation. Father God, open the eyes of his understanding that he will be transformed by the renewing of his mind. Your Word tells us in Philippians 2:5 to let the mind of Christ be within us, and I pray that _____ will take on the mindset of Christ for his benefit. LORD, create in _____ a clean heart and renew the right spirit within him. In Jesus' name. Amen.

PRAYER REQUESTS/PRAISE REPORTS

_____

_____

_____

_____

_____

_____

_____

ACTION PLAN

PRAISE — Praise God for providing positive role models for the one(s) you've prayed for.

REFLECT — Reflect on a time when God's righteousness helped you.

ACT — Ask the Holy Spirit to renew the right spirit within you.

YIELD — Meditate on the scriptures below.

SUPPORTING SCRIPTURES

Philippians 2:5 – Let this mind be in you, which was also in Christ Jesus:

1 Corinthians 15:33 – Be not deceived: evil communications corrupt good manners.

Proverbs 11:3 – The integrity of the upright will guide them, but the crookedness of the treacherous will destroy them.

Day 29

Day 30
LOVE

It has been said that love is the greatest gift ever given to mankind. Everyone has been given the capacity to receive it and share it with others. That same great gift has a known enemy which seeks to undermine it. Satan knows that if he can sabotage love in any capacity, he can block the flow of this gift. Jesus reminds us of the importance of love by telling us that love is the greatest precept of all. God's love is above all and the enemy is defenseless against it.

There are subtle ways that we show how much we love something or someone, and time is one of the most telling ways. Wherever we invest our time and energy will usually be a reflection of what we love. If something is important to us, we tend to show it by the way we invest in it. The bible tells us that our hearts are connected to the things we treasure.

Day 30

1 Corinthians 13 tells us that we can have all kinds of great gifts and do amazing things, but if we do not have love, we have nothing. It is also important to be mindful of whom and what we choose to love. For example, in the parable that Jesus gave of the rich young ruler in Mark 10:17-31, the young man chose to love his riches over the opportunity of a love for Christ. If the love we claim does not allow God to be our first love, then we are not experiencing true love, for God is love. Let us pray for God's love to be demonstrated through the lives of those that we pray for.

I exhort therefore, that, first of all, supplications, prayers, intercessions, and giving of thanks, be made for all men; 1 Timothy 2:1

PRAYER

Abba Father, I bless You for being the God of love. I lift _____ before Your throne of grace. LORD, fill _____ with Your unfailing love. Teach _____ to love You with all of his heart, mind, soul, and strength, and show _____ how to demonstrate Your love to others just as he would love himself. LORD, surround _____ with people who love him and support him. Father God, Your Word says in 1 John 3:18 that we should not love by the words of our mouth alone, but by our deeds and in truth. I pray that _____ will love in deed and in truth. I plead the blood of Jesus against any hindrances to the love that You provide. Holy Spirit, crown _____ with grace and wisdom to love himself, his wife, his children, his family, and all who are connected to him. In Jesus' name. Amen.

PRAYER REQUESTS/PRAISE REPORTS

_____

_____

_____

_____

_____

Day 30

ACTION PLAN

PRAISE — Praise God for loving the one(s) you've prayed for.

REFLECT — Reflect on the love God has for you.

ACT — Listen to one of your favorite songs about God's love.

YIELD — Meditate on the scriptures below.

SUPPORTING SCRIPTURES

Ephesians 5:25 – Husbands, love your wives, as Christ loved the church and gave himself up for her,

1 Corinthians 13:4-7 – Love is patient, love is kind and is not jealous; love does not brag and is not arrogant, does not act unbecomingly; it does not seek its own, is not provoked, does not take into account a wrong suffered, does not rejoice in unrighteousness, but rejoices with the truth; bears all things, believes all things, hopes all things, endures all things.

1 John 4:11 – Beloved, if God so loved us, we ought also to love one another.

Day 31
SURRENDER

Have you ever sat down and wrote out your dreams and plans? Maybe you are the type of person who starts each year with a new resolution to get in shape, save money, or level up in your business. And just when you hit your stride and things start coming together, something unexpected happens and puts you right back to where you started or even farther back than you were when you made the decision to start in the first place. How does that sudden interruption make you feel? Helpless?? Out of control???

Sometimes, our greatest wakeup calls come to us when we realize that things are beyond us. The moment we realize that our plans might be our own, but it is God Himself who orchestrates our true progress – this is the moment of surrender. This is the moment when we are willing to see God's vision for our lives and we are willing to make His vision

Day 31

our compass and guide. This is the moment where we release the wheel and allow the Holy Spirit to do the driving for us. Things may not go according to our plan, but as we exchange our will for God's will, things will work together for our good. Surrender is the place where we are content in letting God lead no matter how it looks or no matter how we feel. God has never lost control of anything we have placed in His hands. Let us pray for a life of surrender.

Likewise the Spirit also helpeth our infirmities: for we know not what we should pray for as we ought: but the Spirit itself maketh intercession for us with groanings which cannot be uttered. Romans 8:26

PRAYER

Father God, I come to You in Jesus' name. I give You glory because You are my LORD. I pray for _____ and his life's journey. Father, touch his heart and keep him in the center of Your holy will. LORD, bless _____ to live a life of surrender unto You. Holy Spirit, bless and prosper _____ in all that brings honour to Your name. Father, I pray that _____ will trust You with his whole heart and not lean on his own understanding. LORD, You said in Your Word that those who come to You must believe that You exist, and You will reward those who diligently seek You. LORD, give _____ the faith to believe You and give _____ strength to give You complete control. LORD, give _____ courage to relinquish anything contrary to Your Word and reward _____ for placing full confidence in You. In Jesus' name. Amen.

PRAYER REQUESTS/PRAISE REPORTS

_____

_____

_____

_____

Day 31

ACTION PLAN

PRAISE
Praise God for drawing the one(s) you've prayed for with His love.

REFLECT
Reflect on the moments where you surrendered to God.

ACT
Ask the Holy Spirit to reveal areas in your life where you need to release to Him.

YIELD
Meditate on the scriptures below.

SUPPORTING SCRIPTURES

Romans 12:1 – I beseech you therefore, brethren, by the mercies of God, that ye present your bodies a living sacrifice, holy, acceptable unto God, *which is* your reasonable service.

Luke 9:23 – And he said to *them* all, If any *man* will come after me, let him deny himself, and take up his cross daily, and follow me.

James 4:7 – Submit yourselves therefore to God. Resist the devil, and he will flee from you.

REFLECTIONS

REFLECTIONS

ABOUT THE AUTHOR

Tracy Spencer is a wife and mother of four. She is an ordained minister, psalmist, and entrepreneur, with a passion for serving the needs of her local church and community. Tracy serves in ministry alongside her husband, Apostle Duane Spencer at End Time Ministries of Moreno Valley, CA.

Connect with me on Twitter: @TheTracySpencer
Connect with me on a Facebook: @TSpencerEnterprises
Connect with me on Instagram: @the_tracyspencer
Connect with me via email: TracyGSpencer@gmail.com

Milton Keynes UK
Ingram Content Group UK Ltd.
UKHW022204030324
438776UK00012B/1898

9 780996 680431